This book belongs to

_____

THE OWL AND
THE PUSSYCAT
and Other Nonsense Poems

Illustrated by
Chuck Reasoner

Poems by
EDWARD LEAR

The Unicorn Publishing House
New Jersey

Edward Lear
1812-1888

Edward Lear was a master at telling funny and curious stories. His characters have delighted children for generations. This book contains three of his most popular poems:

THE OWL AND THE PUSSYCAT

THE JUMBLIES

THE POBBLE WHO HAS NO TOES

This edition is dedicated to his memory and to all the wonderful poetry he has left us— just for the fun of it.

The accompanying image is drawn from a poem Edward Lear wrote about himself. The cat was named "Old Foss," and was Mr. Lear's dearest friend and companion.

The Owl and the Pussy-Cat

I

The Owl and the Pussy-Cat went to sea
    In a beautiful pea-green boat,
They took some honey, and plenty of money,
    Wrapped up in a five-pound note.
The Owl looked up to the stars above,
    And sang to a small guitar,
"O lovely Pussy! O Pussy, my love,
    What a beautiful Pussy you are,
        You are,
        You are!
What a beautiful Pussy you are!"

II

Pussy said to the Owl, "You elegant fowl!
How charmingly sweet you sing!
O let us be married! too long we have tarried:
But what shall we do for a ring?"
They sailed away for a year and a day,
To the land where the Bong-tree grows,
And there in a wood a Piggy-wig stood,
With a ring at the end of his nose,
His nose,
His nose,
With a ring at the end of his nose.

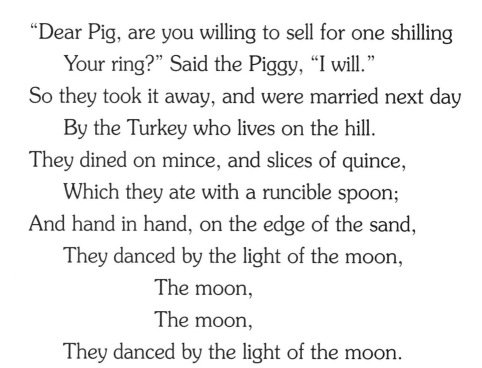

III

"Dear Pig, are you willing to sell for one shilling
   Your ring?" Said the Piggy, "I will."
So they took it away, and were married next day
   By the Turkey who lives on the hill.
They dined on mince, and slices of quince,
   Which they ate with a runcible spoon;
And hand in hand, on the edge of the sand,
   They danced by the light of the moon,
         The moon,
         The moon,
   They danced by the light of the moon.

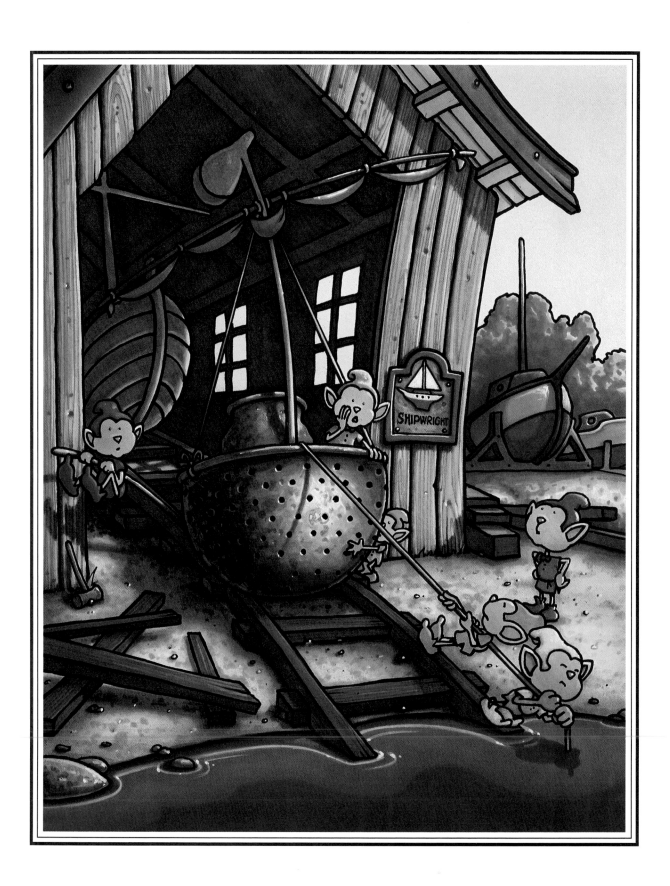

The Jumblies

I

They went to sea in a Sieve, they did,
    In a Sieve they went to sea:
In spite of all their friends could say,
On a winter's morn, on a stormy day,
    In a Sieve they went to sea!
And when the Sieve turned round and round,
And every one cried, "You'll all be drowned!"
They called aloud, "Our Sieve ain't big,
But we don't care a button! we don't care a fig!
    In a Sieve we'll go to sea!"
    Far and few, far and few,
    Are the lands where the Jumblies live;
Their heads are green, and their hands are blue,
    And they went to sea in a Sieve.

II

They sailed away in a Sieve, they did,
　　In a Sieve they sailed so fast,
With only a beautiful pea-green veil
Tied with a riband by way of a sail,
　　To a small tobacco-pipe mast;
And every one said, who saw them go,
"O won't they be soon upset, you know!
For the sky is dark, and the voyage is long,
And happen what may, it's extremely wrong
　　　In a Sieve to sail so fast!"
　　　Far and few, far and few,
　　　Are the lands where the Jumblies live;
Their heads are green, and their hands are blue,
　　And they went to sea in a Sieve.

III

The water it soon came in, it did,
    The water it soon came in;
So to keep them dry, they wrapped their feet
In a pinky paper all folded neat,
    And they fastened it down with a pin.
And they passed the night in a crockery-jar,
And each of them said, "How wise we are!
Though the sky be dark, and the voyage be long,
Yet we never can think we were rash or wrong,
      While round in our Sieve we spin!"
      Far and few, far and few,
      Are the lands where the Jumblies live;
Their heads are green, and their hands are blue,
    And they went to sea in a Sieve.

IV

And all night long they sailed away;
    And when the sun went down,
They whistled and warbled a moony song
To the echoing sound of a coppery gong,
    In the shade of the mountains brown.
"O Timballo! How happy we are,
When we live in a sieve and a crockery-jar,
And all night long in the moonlight pale,
We sail away with a pea-green sail,
      In the shade of the mountains brown!"
      Far and few, far and few,
      Are the lands where the Jumblies live;
Their heads are green, and their hands are blue,
    And they went to sea in a Sieve.

V

They sailed to the Western Sea, they did.
    To a land all covered with trees,
And they bought an Owl, and a useful Cart,
And a pound of Rice, and a Cranberry Tart,
    And a hive of silvery Bees.
And they bought a Pig, and some green Jack-daws,
And a lovely Monkey with lollipop paws,
And forty bottles of Ring-Bo-Ree,
        And no end of Stilton Cheese.
        Far and few, far and few,
        Are the lands where the Jumblies live;
Their heads are green, and their hands are blue,
    And they went to sea in a Sieve.

VI

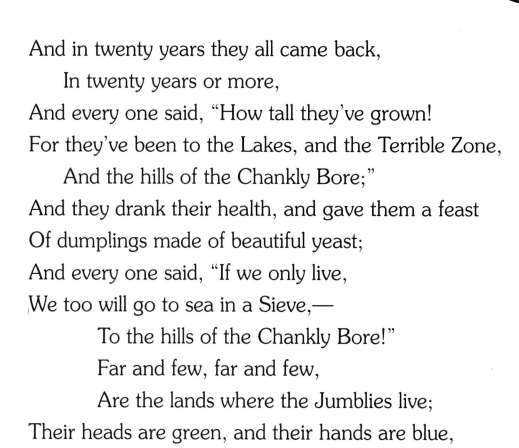

And in twenty years they all came back,
    In twenty years or more,
And every one said, "How tall they've grown!
For they've been to the Lakes, and the Terrible Zone,
    And the hills of the Chankly Bore;"
And they drank their health, and gave them a feast
Of dumplings made of beautiful yeast;
And every one said, "If we only live,
We too will go to sea in a Sieve,—
        To the hills of the Chankly Bore!"
        Far and few, far and few,
        Are the lands where the Jumblies live;
Their heads are green, and their hands are blue,
    And they went to sea in a Sieve.

The Pobble Who Has No Toes

I

The Pobble who has no toes
    Had once as many as we;
When they said, "Some day you may lose them all;"
    He replied,—"Fish fiddle de-dee!"
And his Aunt Jobiska made him drink,
Lavender water tinged with pink,
For she said, "The World in general knows
There's nothing so good for a Pobble's toes!"

II

The Pobble who has no toes,
    Swam across the Bristol Channel;
But before he set out he wrapped his nose,
    In a piece of scarlet flannel.
For his Aunt Jobiska said, "No harm
"Can come to his toes if his nose is warm;
"And it's perfectly known that a Pobble's toes
"Are safe,—provided he minds his nose."

III

The Pobble swam fast and well,
     And when boats or ships came near him
He tinkledy-binkledy-winkled a bell,
     So that all the world could hear him.
And all the Sailors and Admirals cried,
When they saw him nearing the further side,
"He has gone to fish, for his Aunt Jobiska's
"Runcible Cat with crimson whiskers!"

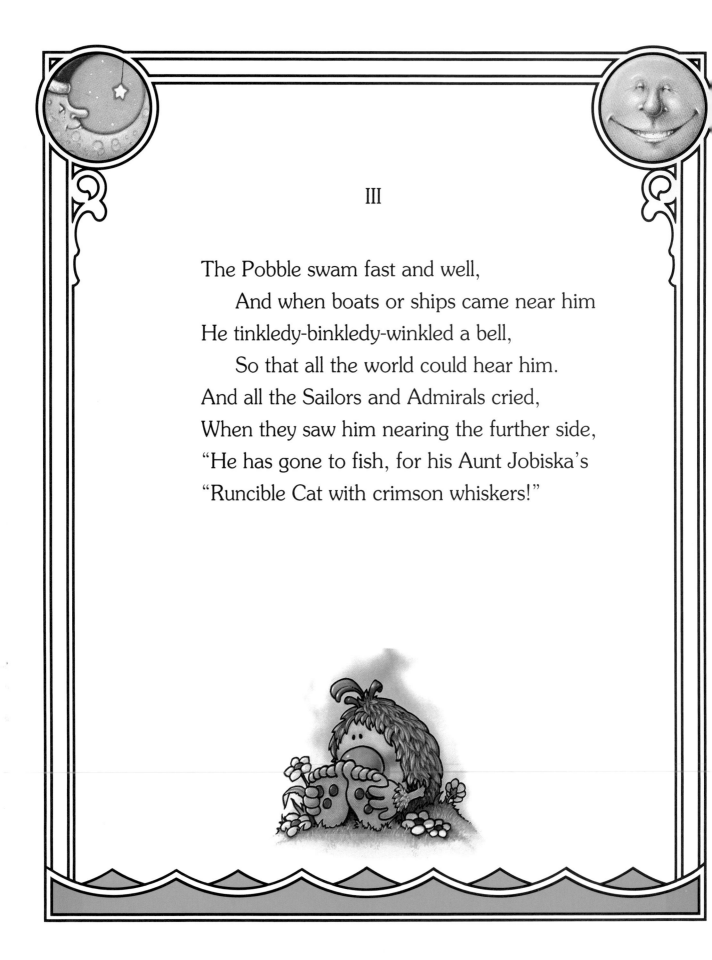

IV

But before he touched the shore,
    The shore of the Bristol Channel,
A sea-green Porpoise carried away
    His wrapper of scarlet flannel.
And when he came to observe his feet,
Formerly garnished with toes so neat,
His face at once became forlorn
On perceiving that all his toes were gone!

V

And nobody ever knew
   From that dark day to the present,
Whoso had taken the Pobble's toes,
   In a manner so far from pleasant.
Whether the shrimps or crawfish gray,
Or crafty Mermaids stole them away—
Nobody knew; and nobody knows
How the Pobble was robbed of his twice five toes!

VI

The Pobble who has no toes
    Was placed in a friendly Bark,
And they rowed him back, and carried him up,
    To his Aunt Jobiska's Park.
And she made him a feast at his earnest wish
Of eggs and buttercups fried with fish;—
And she said,—"It's a fact the whole world knows,
"That Pobbles are happier without their toes."

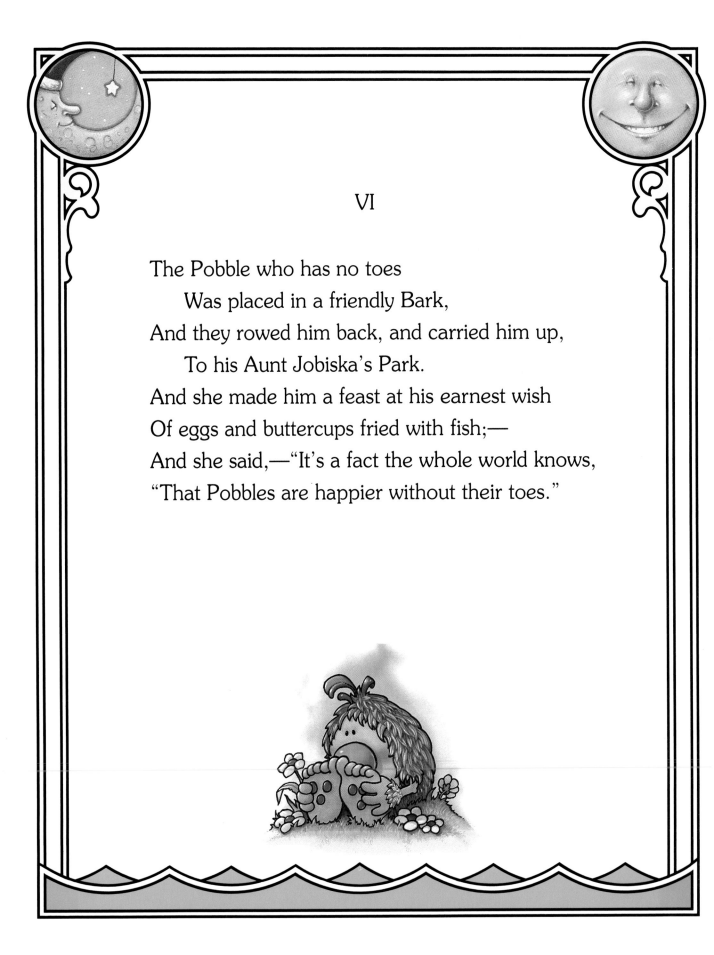

Editor: John Ingram
Art Director: Heidi K.L. Corso
Printed in U.S.A.
© 1990 The Unicorn Publishing House. All Rights Reserved
Art Work © 1990 Chuck Reasoner. All Rights Reserved
No copyrighted elements of this book may be reproduced in whole or in part, by any means, without written permission.
For information contact, Jean L. Scrocco,
Unicorn Publishing House, 120 American Road, Morris Plains, NJ 07950

Printing History 15 14 13 12 11 10 9 8 7 6 5 4 3 2 1

Library of Congress Cataloging-in-Publication Data

Lear, Edward, 1812-1888.
The Owl and the Pussycat and Other Nonsense Poems/illustrated by Chuck Reasoner: poems by Edward Lear.
p. cm. -- (Through the Magic Window)
Summary: Presents four illustrated poems of Edward Lear: "Lines to a Young Lady," "The Jumblies," "The Owl and the Pussycat,"
and "The Pobble Who Has No Toes."
ISBN 0-88101-096-0: $9.95
1. Children's poetry, English. 2. Nonsense-verses, English. [1. Nonsense verses. 2. English poetry.] I. Reasoner, Charles, ill.
II. Title. III. Series.
PR4879.L2A6   1990b   89-39473
821'.8--dc20   CIP
                                                                                                      AC

Other Delightful Stories
Richly Illustrated in Our
Through The Magic Window Series:

THE ELF AND THE DORMOUSE

WYNKEN, BLYNKEN, AND NOD

THE EMPEROR'S NEW CLOTHES

PETER COTTONTAIL'S SURPRISE